Summer Survival

(or What to Do When You're Bored)

Nancy E. Velon

Illustrated by Debra Teel

Scott, Foresman and Company
Glenview, Illinois   London

 **Good Year Books**
are available for preschool through grade 12 and for every basic curriculum subject plus many enrichment areas. For more Good Year Books, contact your local bookseller or educational dealer. For a complete catalog with information about other Good Year Books, please write:

Good Year Books
Department GYB
1900 East Lake Avenue
Glenview, Illinois 60025

Dedication
To Moms and Dads everywhere who've
ever heard "Now what can I do?"
and
to my Mom who has the best collection
of "odds and ends" of anyone.
Thank you for letting me be creative.

Copyright © 1990 Nancy E. Velon.
All Rights Reserved.
Printed in the United States of America.

1 2 3 4 5 6 PAT 95 94 93 92 91 90

ISBN 0-673-46267-6

No part of this book may be reproduced in any form or by any means, except those portions intended for classroom use, without permission in writing from the publisher.

Contents

June

1. Call a Friend 1
2. News Reporter 1
3. Car Safety Kit 2
4. Climb a Tree 2
5. Take a Walk 3
6. Spooky Stories 3
7. Face Painting 4
8. The Best Backyard 4
9. Reading 5
10. Masks 5
11. Be a Good Observer 6
12. Making a Rubbing 7
13. Stuffed Animals 7
14. Flower or Weed Vases 8
15. How Do You Measure Up? 9
16. Poetry—Haiku 10
17. Summertime Parfait 11
18. Dots and Dashes 11
19. Let's Pretend 12
20. Creature Drawings 12
21. Batter Up! 13
22. Modeling Dough 14
23. Music 14
24. Ice Cube Lasso 15
25. Count in German 15
26. Bubble Gum Blowing 16
27. Robby Robot 17
28. Soap Sculpture 17
29. Fractured Fairy Tale 18
30. Matching Socks 18

July

1. Lunch Surprise 19
2. Summer Camp 19
3. Taking a Survey 20
4. Celebration Flag 21
5. King or Queen for a Day 21
6. Shoe Shine 22
7. Rainy Day Blues 22
8. Fingerprint Art 23
9. Toothpicks 23
10. Signs of the Zodiac 24
11. Strawberry Lemon Slush 25
12. Wood Tag 25
13. Crystal Garden 26
14. Shell Identification 27

15	Poetry—Limerick	27
16	Decorated Plant Pots	28
17	Tongue Twister	29
18	Junk Sculptures	30
19	Reflections	31
20	The Money Jar	31
21	Cent Facts	32
22	Sand Pictures	33
23	Count in Spanish	33
24	Journal Writing	34
25	Knox Blocks Zoo	34
26	Sponge Painting	35
27	Creepy Critters	36
28	It Really Bugs Me!	37
29	Collecting Coins	37
30	Gramblers	38
31	Balloon Volleyball	38

August

1	Jigsaw Puzzle	39
2	Wheels	39
3	People Search	40
4	Mold Garden	41
5	Count in French	41
6	Your Perfect Bedroom	42
7	Magazine Montage	42
8	Blueprints	43
9	Turn Off the Lights	44
10	Toothpick Design	44
11	Nature Art	45
12	Riddles	46
13	Straw Painting	47
14	Flour Clay	47
15	Clouds	48
16	Poetry—Cinquain	49
17	Orange Freeze	49
18	Word Pictures	50
19	Recycled Greeting Cards	50
20	Magnet Magic	51
21	Seed Pictures	52
22	Musical Glasses	52
23	Scavenger Hunt	53
24	Baker's Clay	54
25	Hot-Dish Trivet	55
26	Tangrams	56
27	Make an Organic Garden	57
28	Board Games	58
29	Good Luck Box	58
30	Back to School	59
31	Hang Loose	60

1
Call a Friend

Are you lonely? Call a friend.

Keep your conversation short. Don't tie up the phone in case other people need to use it.

Is someone in the hospital? Give the person a cheery call. BUT do
    not
        talk
            too
                long.

A person in the hospital probably needs to rest.

Call Grandma and Grandpa just to let them know you are thinking about them. BUT never call long distance without first getting permission.

JUNE

2
News Reporter

Be a news reporter for your block.

Keep your ears open for something interesting to share with other kids.

You might want to keep a notebook of things you learn.

Decide how you want to report what you discover:

    ☆ make a poster?
    ☆ hand out computer-printed copies?
    ☆ give out hand-printed flyers?
    ☆ build a platform and deliver a speech?

Remember the five important questions to answer in a news article:
    Who?
    What?
    Where?
    When?
    Why?

3
Car Safety Kit

It's always a good idea to have a safety kit in the car in case of an emergency. Here's a safety kit that you can put together by yourself.

Materials:
- shoe box
- paint
- glue
- reflector tape
- ribbon, string, or yarn
- first-aid supplies: adhesive bandages, gauze, tape, antiseptic, iodine

Start by painting the box. When it dries, glue the ribbon, yarn, or string to the bottom of the box. The ribbon, yarn, or string should be long enough to tie around the box.

Make the letters S, L, O, and W from reflector tape. Press the letters onto the top of the box to spell the word SLOW. Tell Mom or Dad to place the top of the box in the back window as a warning to other drivers if your car ever breaks down or gets a flat tire.

Fill the box with first-aid supplies.

Place the box in the trunk of the car or under one of the seats.

JUNE

4
Climb a Tree

How does the world look from 10 feet up?

Climb a tree and observe everything below you.

Make sure the tree is strong enough to hold you. Take care not to harm the tree that you decide to climb.

Ask Dad if he had a tree house when he was a little boy. Ask him to tell you about his tree house or about the places he would go to climb trees. Invite Dad to climb a tree with you.

Invite a friend to climb your favorite tree with you.

5 Take a Walk

Walking is great exercise.

You can go for a walk at any age.

The only equipment you need is good walking shoes.

Be a good observer when you take a walk. Notice the environment around you. What can you find that you never saw before?

Take a walk with a friend.

Walk in your neighborhood.

Walk two blocks each way.

Count the number of houses.
    How many of the houses have just one story?
    How many of the houses have two or more stories?

How many different colors can you count on the houses you see?

Tell your friend which house is your favorite. Why?

---

6 Spooky Stories

JUNE

Did you ever have a sleepover and someone wanted to tell scary stories? Write down the sentences below and save them for your next sleepover. Then use them to begin your own spooky stories.

    My mother told me never to open the door at the end of the long hallway. But one day I did, and . . .

    On a moonless night, I took a shortcut through the old cemetery. Suddenly I heard a noise. I turned around very slowly and saw . . .

    One night I awoke with a start. Something—or someone—was scratching at my window. I tiptoed over, heard nothing and saw nothing, and so I went back to bed. Scratch, scratch, I heard again. I went back to the window, and this time . . .

    The man next door brought us a scary jack-o'-lantern that he had carved. We put it on a table that was out of the way so we wouldn't have to look at it. But every once in awhile I sneaked a peek. It seemed to me that the jack-o'-lantern was changing, turning into a . . .

7 Face Painting

Would you like to be a clown, an Indian, a monster, an old lady, an old man?

Collect the materials listed below. Then go outside or in the garage and try painting your face.

Materials:

    mirror   paint brushes   an old mop
    petroleum jelly   old nylon stockings   construction paper
    food coloring   yarn   play hats and clothing
    flour   water   funny shoes
    water color paints   old towels

To make finger paint for your face, you can mix a few drops of food coloring into a small amount of petroleum jelly. Or you can add a few drops of water to water color paints and then use a small brush to paint your face.

You can put on some flour to make your face white.

Put an old stocking over your head and become a scary monster.

Add some extra hair with an old wig, strips of construction paper curled up, an old mop head, or lengths of yarn.

Dress up in play clothes and have a party or a parade.

8 The Best Backyard

Think of your backyard.

How would you change it to make it the best backyard in your town?
    What would you add?
    What would you take away?
    Would your backyard have a secret place?
    Would it be colorful?
    Would adults like to play there?

Make a drawing of your best backyard.

Materials:
    large piece of newsprint or drawing paper
    pencil
    ruler
    crayons or markers

9 Reading

Reading can take you to faraway places.

Reading can introduce you to new friends.

Reading can help you learn how to do something you want to do.

Reading is a relaxing thing to do before you go to sleep after a busy day.

Reading is just plain fun!

Try keeping a record of all the books you read during the summer.

Make a book jacket for each book you read.

Make a drawing of your favorite character in the book.

JUNE

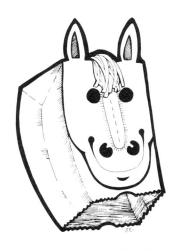

10 Masks

With a mask, you can pretend to be anyone you want to be.

Paper Bag Mask. Decorate a paper grocery bag with construction paper, crepe paper, or tissue paper to make an attractive mask. Carefully cut out eye holes in the bag so that you can see. Add frayed yarn, a mop, or an old wig for the hair.

Box Mask. Find a box large enough and deep enough to cover your face. Cut down the corners of the box about six inches. You can use any extra cardboard for ears. Cut holes for the eyes and mouth. To make the face of the mask, cover the box with construction paper and add pieces of yarn, felt, or interesting scraps of other materials.

Paper Plate Mask. Get a large paper plate and cut out holes for your eyes and nose. Then paint or decorate the plate in any way you choose.

11
Be a Good Observer

How well can you remember what you see?

Get a lid from a large cardboard box (a cookie sheet or a large cake pan will work, too).

Collect 25 different things, each one no larger than your hand.

Place all the items in the box lid.

Let a friend look at the things for two minutes. Use a timer (or a watch with a second hand) to keep track of the time. Then take away the box lid.

Ask your friend to tell you or make a list of all the items he or she can remember seeing.

You might do this with several people (one at a time) and give a small prize to the person who remembers the most.

You can play a similar game alone.

Go into a room in your home and look around for two minutes.

Leave the room and list all the things you saw on a piece of paper. Then return to the room and notice all the things you forgot to put on your list.

Choose a color and then look for all the things in the room of that color.

Here's a hint for remembering more items: When you look at an object in the room, think about what it is used for.

12
Making a Rubbing

Rubbing is an old art. To make a rubbing, all you have to do is place a piece of paper over a surface and rub across the paper with a pencil, hard crayon, or piece of charcoal.

When the rubbing is finished, the design on the surface that you rubbed appears on the paper in a light and dark pattern. The final effect depends on how hard you rubbed and what it was that you rubbed.

You can make rubbings indoors or outdoors. Look around the house for something with a raised design. Coins work well, but be sure to ask permission before you use anything breakable.

Put the paper on top of the design. Rub a pencil, crayon, or piece of charcoal lightly over the paper. Watch the design appear.

Now go outside and find a fairly flat rock. Put a piece of paper on the rock and rub lightly. Look at the design. Try making rubbings of trees, leaves, and different kinds of wood.

You can make rubbings of names etched in the sidewalk. The gravestones in a cemetery are also great for making rubbings.

13
Stuffed Animals

How many stuffed animals do you have?

A rainy day is a great time to play with your animals.

Have you given them all names?

Which one is your favorite?

Invite a friend to bring over his or her stuffed animals. Does your friend have one stuffed animal that you really like? Ask if you can keep the animal overnight. Let your friend keep one of your animals overnight, too.

14
Flower or Weed Vases

Materials:
- glass bottles: salad dressing, catsup, etc.
- white glue
- yarn in different colors
- toothpick

Cover the top inch of the bottle with glue. Wind yarn around the top of the bottle, keeping the layers close together. Cover the next inch down on the bottle with glue and continue winding the yarn.

If you want to change yarn colors, cut the yarn you're winding and press the end into the glue. Use a toothpick to tuck the beginning of the new yarn color at the end of the old one. Add a drop of glue at the place where the two yarns meet, and use the toothpick to press the ends down for a few minutes.

Continue applying glue to the bottle and winding yarn around it until the whole bottle is covered. At first, the glue will look white and messy, but it will dry clear and invisible.

When the vase is finished and dry, fill it with flowers from your garden. If you make several vases, you can collect weeds and arrange them in your decorated bottles. Some weeds do not need water. They will dry and last for months.

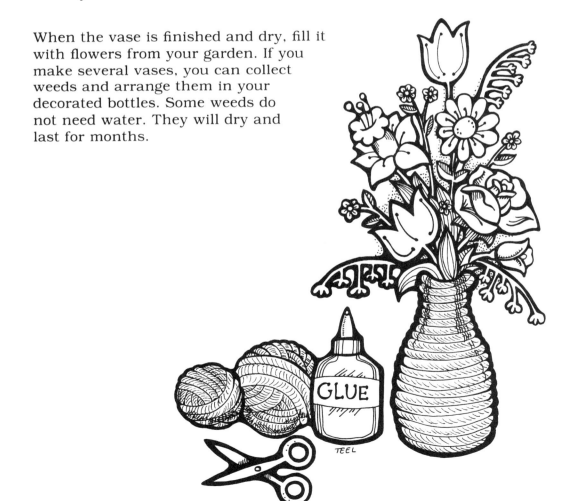

JUNE

15
How Do You Measure Up?

Ask Mom if you may borrow the tape measure from her sewing basket. Be sure to return it.

Find your measurements. You might need a friend to help.

I am _____ inches tall.

The distance around my head measures _____ inches.

My right foot is _____ inches long.

My left thumb is _____ inches long.

The distance from my elbow to the tip of my little finger is _____ inches.

My nose is _____ inches long.

My waist is _____ inches around.

The distance around my right wrist is _____ inches.

It is _____ inches from my shoulder to my elbow.

The distance from my waist to the floor measures _____ inches.

Now repeat these measurements in centimeters.

16
Poetry — Haiku

Poems can have many different meanings. They can be put together in a variety of ways. They may follow a specific pattern or have no pattern at all. They may be long or short. They may rhyme or not rhyme.

Haiku (pronounced hi-coo) poems are a special kind of Japanese poem that paints a word picture of one thing. Usually the subject of a haiku is something in nature.

The haiku follows a strict pattern. It always has three lines, and each line must have a certain number of syllables:

Line 1 has five syllables.

Line 2 has seven syllables.

Line 3 has five syllables.

A syllable is a part of a word that has a separate sound. For example, the word "today" has two syllables: to day.
                                                    1   2

Here's a haiku I wrote about summer.

>Summer hot and warm,
>Birds calling, bees buzzing,
>Breezes blow all day.
>
>   Nancy E. Velon

Now create your own haiku poems. Hint: You may find it easier to count syllables by clapping at each one.

Summertime Parfait

You can make a delicious, healthy summertime treat. This recipe will serve four people.

Ingredients:
    ⅓ cup plain, low-fat yogurt
    1 small banana, peeled and mashed
    1 teaspoon sugar
    ¼ teaspoon cinnamon
    1⅓ cups diced cantaloupe
    1½ cups blueberries

Mix together the yogurt, banana, sugar, and cinnamon in a small bowl.

Arrange the cantaloupe in the bottoms of four parfait glasses. You can also use regular glass fruit dishes.

Spoon about 1 tablespoon of the yogurt mixture over the cantaloupe in each glass. Top with the blueberries and another tablespoon of the yogurt mixture. Chill until serving time.

Reproduced with permission.
©*Children's Help Your Heart Cookbook*, 1980.
Copyright American Heart Association.

Dots and Dashes

Samuel Morse invented the telegraph in 1837. He then created the Morse Code to use for sending messages by wire.

Each letter in the code is made up of a different combination of dots and dashes. You can write the code. You can speak the code. You can tap it out with a pencil. You can even blink it out in the dark with a flashlight.

Here's the Morse Code:

A	.—	H	....	O	———	V	...—
B	—...	I	..	P	.——.	W	.——
C	—.—.	J	.———	Q	——.—	X	—..—
D	—..	K	—.—	R	.—.	Y	—.——
E	.	L	.—..	S	...	Z	——..
F	..—.	M	——	T	—		
G	——.	N	—.	U	..—		

When you send a message to a friend in Morse Code, he or she must also know the code in order to figure out your message.

19
Let's Pretend

If you had a magic lamp, what would you wish for?

Think of ten wishes. The only thing you cannot wish for is more wishes!

Write down your ten wishes and your reasons for choosing them.

_____
_____
_____
_____
_____
_____
_____
_____
_____
_____

JUNE

20
Creature Drawings

Materials:
  paper
  pencil
  pen
  colored pencils
  markers

Draw several shapes on a piece of paper.

Add parts to each shape, turning it into an interesting or silly creature.

Draw some more shapes. Then ask a friend to turn your shapes into creatures.

21
Batter Up!

Can you find these baseball batting champions in the puzzle grid below? The names are spelled forward, backward, up, down, and diagonally.

AARON	FOXX	KELL	MUSIAL	TORRE
BOGGS	FURILLO	LOMBARDI	OLIVA	VAUGHAN
BUCKNER	GEHRIG	LANSFORD	PARKER	WALKER
CAREW	GOSLIN	MADLOCK	ROBINSON	WILLIAMS
CLEMENTE	HEILMAN	MANTLE	ROSE	WILSON
DIMAGGIO	HERNANDEZ	MAYS	RUTH	YASTRZEMSKI

```
Y B S N R O H S S M A D L O C K S N R G
A O L I V A W I L L I A M S L G L O O N
S U E E G C M B R E Y M R Y G A B S A I
T D C L E M E N T E N T N O I I L L S L
R R T K O G O O D M A N B S N I I I P
Z E D N A N R E H S H N U S N T G W V P
E A S R I K E L L I G M O R R W O C A A
M U M A G E O T H S U N H D E E A R D R
S S F R N S L N T L A A I C G N K N R K
K M O I Y O L A U E V D S K I O K L E E
I A L O U R I M R R R P S M R N N C A R
T A T T E R R A V A C B I G H R O N U W
K M I Z E I U E B C A R E W E E S O A B
C A S H K O F M T N N Y W G G V N S C N
H Y L U O D O M A T T I N G L Y I N E H
S S O W C L L P A Q S I R O R U B H T A
U N H E I L M A N N R E I S E R O O N F
N S E V A R G R A H R Y T R A C R J O E
A M E D W I C K E L A N S F O R D X F Y
M R D I M A G G I O G R E D N A X E L A
```

JUNE

Bonus Game: Can you find these additional baseball stars? Try working with a friend.

ALOU	GOODMAN	MANUSH	MIZE	TERRY
CARTY	GROAT	MATTINGLY	OLIVER	VERNON
CASH	JOHNSON	MEDWICK	SIMMONS	WANER
GEHRINGER	KALINE			

22
Modeling Dough

You can make many interesting things from modeling dough. You can even make your own dough! Here's the recipe.

Ingredients:
- 1 cup cornstarch
- 1 cup salt
- 1 cup cold water

Use a large spoon to mix the cornstarch, salt, and water together in a bowl.

Allow the mixture to set until it does not stick to your fingers.

If you like, you can add food coloring to the mixture to make colored modeling dough.

Use cookie cutters to cut the dough into shapes. If you plan to hang your shapes, punch holes in them with a toothpick or pencil before they dry. Let your shapes dry completely before handling them.

JUNE

23
Music

Music is good for enjoyment. It can help you relax. You also can exercise to music.

Listen to the radio, records, tapes, and compact discs.

A song is a poem set to music. Choose your favorite tune and write a poem for it. Then see if you can make up an original tune for a song.

Ask a friend to write a poem for your favorite tune. Then compare songs.

Write a poem with your friend. Then make up a tune to fit the poem.

24
Ice Cube Lasso

Can you pick up an ice cube without touching it? Here's how to do a trick for your friends.

Place an ice cube in a small bowl of water. Make a loop in one end of a piece of string about 12 inches long. Lower the loop onto the ice cube. Make sure that the loop lies flat on top of the ice.

Now sprinkle some salt on both the loop and the ice cube.

Count to ten slowly. Then pull up gently on the string. You will lift the ice cube out of the water!

Here's how the trick works: When you sprinkle salt on the ice cube, the ice around the salt melts. Then, very quickly, the ice cube causes the melted ice to refreeze. When this happens, the string is frozen into the ice cube.

25
Count in German

Did any of your ancestors come from Germany?

Do you have any German-speaking friends?

Learning a foreign language can be fun. Try counting to ten in German. The middle column shows the German words for the numbers from 1 to 10. The right-hand column will help you pronounce the German words.

1	eins	īns		6	sechs	zeks
2	zwei	tsvī		7	sieben	zeé-ben
3	drei	drī		8	acht	ahkht
4	vier	feer		9	neun	noyn
5	fünf	feunf		10	zehn	tsehn

26
Bubble Gum Blowing

Have you ever wondered how we get bubble gum? Bubble gum begins just like regular gum. All chewing gum comes from the sapodilla tree. Workers remove the gum base—called "chicle"—by slitting the bark of the trees.

The milky white chicle is collected in buckets at the bottom of the tree. Then it is boiled in large pots, formed into blocks, and sent to a factory.

At the factory, the chicle is cleaned and purified. Then it is mixed with flavorings like peppermint or spearmint. The flavored gum is rolled into a thin sheet and cut into pieces by automatic cutting machines. The pieces are then packaged and sealed by special machines, loaded onto trucks, and delivered to stores.

Bubble gum is mixed with other ingredients (including rubber) to make it more elastic. Bubble gum must be more elastic so that you can blow bubbles with it.

How big a bubble do you think you can blow? Why not have a bubble-blowing contest with a friend or two? It's best to hold the contest outside and to have a washcloth handy.

Make sure everyone starts out with the same amount of bubble gum.

Chew the gum well. Then see who can blow the biggest bubble.

BLOW!   BLOW!   BLOW!   BLOW!

27
Robby Robot

A robot is a machine that can do many things that people do. But a robot cannot think for itself. It must be told what to do—programmed.

If you had a robot, what would you program it to do?

Think of as many interesting things as you can. Try to think of something that no has ever asked a robot to do before.

You can build your own robot out of old scrap boxes of different sizes. Use buttons, bottle tops, wire, and other objects to make a face and other features for your robot.

28
Soap Sculpture

Did you ever stop to think that there might be some figure hidden in your bar of soap? Here's how to become a soap sculptor and discover all the shapes that can hide in soap.

Materials:
  bar of soap
     (Ivory works well because it is soft)
  carving tools
     (a small kitchen knife or a plastic knife)
  spoon
  fork
  large nail
  paper
  pencil

Before you begin, draw a picture on paper of what you would like your soap carving to be. You can even trace an outline of the shape on both sides of the bar of soap.

After tracing the outline onto the bar of soap, use the knife to shave off any soap you don't want *a little at a time.* Keep removing bits of soap until you have the exact shape you want.

If you accidentally split the bar of soap while cutting it, just make a smaller shape. If you want lines on your shape, you can make them by scraping the soap with the prongs of a fork. A spoon can help you hollow out an area.

For a smooth finish on your sculpture, gently rub the surface of the soap with a damp cloth. If you want to hang your sculpture, *very carefully* work a nail back and forth until you create a hole in the soap.

29
Fractured Fairy Tale

Think of one of your favorite fairy tales. Now think of ways to change the story so that it is very different.

Here's an example:

Goldilocks and the Five Bears

One day, Goldilocks took her backpack and set off to visit Aunt Jennifer. When she arrived at Aunt Jennifer's house, no one was home. So Goldilocks crawled through a window and went inside.

Before long, five bears knocked at the door and wanted to come in. Goldilocks let them come inside. Since there was no food in Aunt Jennifer's house, Goldilocks and the five bears ordered pizza.

You can finish this story any way you like. Then write your own versions of other favorite fairy tales.

30
Matching Socks

Does your clothes washer or dryer eat socks? Where could the missing socks go?

Start by matching all the socks in each family member's drawer and in the laundry. Be sure to keep each person's socks separate.

Then go on a search for the missing socks.

1
Lunch Surprise

Do you know of a senior citizen or someone who lives alone on your block?

Make a surprise sack lunch and deliver it to the person. Be sure to get permission from your parents before you go to someone's house.

Think of lunch treats the person might enjoy, not just all your favorites.

Perhaps you could also make a lunch for yourself and eat together with the person you're surprising.

Bon Appétit

2
Summer Camp

Pretend that you have just won the grand prize in a contest. Your reward is two weeks, all expenses paid, at a summer camp.

Plan a summer camp just the way you would like it to be.

Where will the camp be located?

How will you arrive at camp?

Who will go with you?

Will the camp be earthy and rustic?

What comforts will you find?

Will the food be plain or delicious?

Will you sleep in a tent?

What activities will you take part in at camp?

After you plan your perfect summer camp, write a story about it. Then make a large drawing of the camp that would be just right for you.

3
Taking a Survey

Professional poll-takers gather the information that turns into television ratings and other measurements of public opinion.

You can be a poll-taker in your neighborhood. For your poll, think about what you want to learn from the people you will question. Plan to ask each person just one question. Make sure the meaning of the question is clear.

People should be able to answer your question by saying "yes" or "no" or by choosing one of several answers that you give. Here's an example of a yes/no question:

> Do you think kids should have jobs at home?

Here's an example of a multiple-choice question:

> What is your favorite meal?
> a. breakfast
> b. lunch
> c. dinner

Decide how many people you will question and how you will record their answers. Make a list of the people you want to ask.

Take your poll. Be sure to record the answers accurately. Here's how the results might look if you interviewed 20 people:

> People who think kids should have jobs: 15
>
> People who think kids should not have jobs: 5

If you enjoy being a poll-taker, try making a list of questions to ask each person. When you finish asking many people all the questions on your list, tally the answers. Have fun!

Celebration Flag

July 4 is known as Independence Day because this is the day back in 1776 that Congress adopted the Declaration of Independence. It is really the birthday of the United States of America. We usually celebrate July 4 with parades, special programs, and fireworks displays.

You can celebrate Independence Day by making a flag.

Materials:
   newspaper
   red, white, and blue paint
   paint brushes

Open one sheet of newspaper to full size.

Paint the upper left corner—about 1/4 of the newspaper—blue. Allow the paint to dry. Then paint 50 white stars on the blue section. The U. S. flag has one star for each of the 50 states.

Paint the rest of the flag in alternating red and white stripes. Start at the top with a red stripe. Then paint a white stripe below it. Continue until you have 13 alternating red and white stripes filling the rest of the newspaper. The U. S. flag has one stripe for each of the first 13 states.

Let the paint dry completely.

You can hang your flag outside or attach it to your front door.

JULY

King or Queen for a Day

How would you like to be king or queen for just one day?

Make a list of all the things you would like to do—and have done for you—on your special day.

Ask each member of the family to grant you one thing from your list. Then ask your friends to help make your day special in some way.

After you enjoy your special time, treat someone else in your family as king or queen for a day.

21

JULY

6
Shoe Shine

Shoes always look much better when they've been freshly polished.

Materials:
  polish that matches shoe color
  clean cloths or rags
  newspaper

Gather the shoes in your house that need to be polished.

Cover your work area with newspaper.

Dust off the shoes. Then put a little polish on a clean rag and rub it over the shoe. Cover all the shoe parts that can be polished.

Wait a few minutes for the polish to dry. Rub each shoe with a clean cloth until the polish disappears and the shoe looks bright and shiny.

Always remember to use the right polish color for each shoe.

7
Rainy Day Blues

Listen to the rain. How does it sound on the roof? How does it sound on the windowpane? Can you hear a rhythm in the rain?

Think of the ways rain helps us. It waters the flowers and vegetables. It fills the lakes and reservoirs.

When you see it start to rain, set a container outside. When the rain stops, measure the amount of rain in the container with a ruler.

Keep a record of the number of rainy days during the summer. Draw rain drops on the calendar to show each rainy day.

Write a poem about the rain.

⑧ Fingerprint Art

You can turn your fingerprints into pictures of people, insects, animals, and many other things.

Materials:
    inked stamp pad
    paper
    pencil
    felt-tipped pens

Press one finger on the inked stamp pad. Then press your inked finger onto a piece of paper. Let the ink dry on the paper for a few seconds.

Now you are ready to add details. Use a pencil or felt-tipped pen to add a face, legs, arms, or other features to your fingerprint.

To make small fingerprint art pictures that you can frame, use 3x5 index cards instead of sheets of paper.

---

⑨ Toothpicks

Arrange 24 toothpicks in the following pattern:

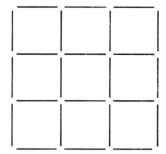

Now take away eight toothpicks so that only two squares are left.

Solution:

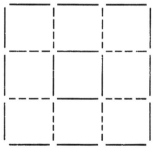

See if your friends can solve this puzzle.

JULY

10 Signs of the Zodiac

When is your birthday? Find the sign of the Zodiac that matches your birthday.

Name	Character	Dates
Aries	ram	March 21-April 19
Taurus	bull	April 20-May 20
Gemini	twins	May 21-June 21
Cancer	crab	June 22-July 22
Leo	lion	July 23-August 22
Virgo	maiden	August 23-September 22
Libra	scales	September 23-October 23
Scorpio	scorpion	October 24-November 21
Sagittarius	archer	November 22-December 21
Capricorn	goat	December 22-January 19
Aquarius	water bearer	January 20-February 18
Pisces	fish	February 19-March 20

Find the signs of the Zodiac that match the birthdays of all the members of your family.

Write a paragraph that tells why a family member is like the Zodiac character that matches his or her birthday.

Which family member is least like his or her Zodiac character? What makes you think the person and the character are so different?

11
Strawberry Lemon Slush

Here's a recipe for a great summertime refresher.

Ingredients:
- 1 cup water
- 1 6-ounce can lemonade concentrate
- 1 10-ounce package frozen strawberries
- 2 cups water
- 4 drops red food coloring
- 2 cups crushed ice
- 6 slices lemon

Put one cup of water, the lemonade concentrate, and the frozen strawberries in a blender container. Adjust the lid. Blend until the strawberries are pureed.

Combine the strawberry mixture with two cups of water and four drops of red food coloring in a pitcher. Stir well. Add the crushed ice and sliced lemon.

This recipe makes six servings.

Reproduced with permission.
©*Children's Help Your Heart Cookbook*, 1980.
Copyright American Heart Association.

12
Wood Tag

This is a good game to play outside with your friends.

Mark out the boundaries in your backyard. Everyone must stay within these boundaries during the game.

Choose someone to be "it" in this special game of tag. All other players are safe from being tagged as long as part of their body is touching wood—a tree, bush, stump, post, fence, etc.

You can vary this game by using metal or stone instead of wood.

13
Crystal Garden

Crystals have flat faces and regular (geometric) shapes. This is because their atoms are arranged in an orderly and repeated pattern.

You can make your own crystal garden.

Materials:
- small pieces (walnut size) of brick
- small pieces of briquette (coal)
- fairly deep glass bowl or jar
- 3 tablespoons bluing
- 3 tablespoons water
- 3 tablespoons noniodized salt
- 1 teaspoon ammonia
- tiny twigs or toothpicks
- food coloring

Place the brick and briquette pieces in the bowl. Prop the twigs between the brick and briquette pieces. Add a little water to the bowl.

Combine the salt, bluing, ammonia, and water in a cup. Mix well.

Slowly pour the mixture in the cup over the brick and briquette pieces in the bowl.

To give color to your garden, sprinkle a few drops of food coloring over the mixture in the bowl.

Place your garden in a warm place where it will not be disturbed.

In a short time, tiny crystals will begin growing. In a few hours, your crystal garden will have odd and interesting shapes.

To keep your garden growing, add one tablespoon of ammonia to it once a week.

14
Shell Identification

Remember your last trip to the beach? Did you collect shells?

Go to the library and take out a book on shells. Sort your shells by kind and size. Use the book to help identify the kinds of shells in your collection.

It might be fun to make a list of all the different kinds you have.

You could make a shell chart on poster board or heavy cardboard. Glue the shells onto the poster board or heavy cardboard. Then write the name of the shell under each one.

Here are two other ideas for having fun with shells. You could make a different kind of shell display by placing your collection in a glass jar. Or you could have a "shell swap" with some of your friends.

15
Poetry—Limerick

A limerick is a humorous type of poem. Since it's just for fun, a limerick doesn't have to be perfect in either rhyme or rhythm.

Once you learn the rules, you'll find that limerick writing is a snap. A limerick has five lines that rhyme like this:

Lines 1, 2, and 5 rhyme.

Lines 3 and 4—the shortest lines—rhyme together.

Most limericks are rather silly. Here's one that I wrote:

There was an old man from Elmhurst
Who thought that his stomach would burst.
He laughed and he cried,
He sighed, then he died.
He never knew what was the worst.

Nancy E. Velon

Now try writing your own limericks. Remember to follow the pattern.

16
Decorated Plant Pots

Many flower and vegetable plants that you buy at a store come in plain plastic or clay pots. Here's how to make those pots look special.

Materials:
- plastic or clay pots
- latex or acrylic paint
- paint brushes
- newspaper
- water

Before you begin, cover your work area with newspaper.

Use leftover latex or acrylic paint to decorate the pots. You can paint a pot entirely in one color, or you can use several colors to create a pretty design.

Be sure to clean your paint brushes carefully so that you can use them again. If you use latex paint, you can clean the brushes with soap and water.

Let the decorated pots dry thoroughly. Then, if they don't have plants in them, add new plants. Surprise Mom with the decorated plant pots, or give one to a friend.

17
Tongue Twister

A tongue twister is a phrase or sentence that is difficult to say due to similar sounds coming right after one another.

How well—and how fast—can you say these tongue twisters?

Practice makes perfect!

Rubber baby buggy bumpers.

She sells seashells by the seashore.

How much wood would a woodchuck chuck if a woodchuck could chuck wood?

Frank threw Fred three free throws.

Six little shavers sheared six sheep.

Round the rough and rugged rocks the ragged rascal ran.

Nine nice nieces nicely nibbled knickknacks.

How much dew would a dewdrop drop if a dewdrop could drop dew?

After you practice these tongue twisters, make up some of your own.

18
Junk Sculptures

Think of all the things that are just sitting on shelves in your home and may one day get thrown out.

See if you can use some of this "junk" to create a sculpture.

Do you have any of the following items?

Materials:
- drinking straws
- playing cards
- hair rollers
- cotton balls and swabs
- clothespins
- nuts and bolts
- empty spools of thread
- empty coffee cans
- popsicle sticks
- corks

To make a junk sculpture, you will also need a piece of wood to serve as a base or platform, some white glue, and, of course, a good imagination!

Begin by gluing different items together on the wood base. You may find that rubber cement or epoxy works better than white glue. Make an interesting figure on the base. Keep adding things on as you work.

You can work alone or with a friend. You might want to add pieces of Styrofoam packing materials. They make very interesting sculptures.

Find a fun place to display your sculpture.

19 Reflections

Mirror, mirror,
In my hand,
Tell me why
I'm the best in the land.

Look into a mirror. Think of ten reasons why you are the best in the land.

It's OK to say good things about yourself.

20 The Money Jar

Saving money can be fun!

Get a gallon jar or a large coffee can with a cover.

At the end of each day, ask each family member to drop all of his or her change into the container.

At the end of one week, count the money. How much money did the family save?

Gather the family together, and decide how to spend the money.
    Ice cream treats?
    Pizza?
    A night of bowling?
    A new board game the whole family can play?
    A long-distance call to Grandma and Grandpa?

Now try to save the family's change for a full month!

JULY

21
Cent Facts

JULY

Get a Lincoln head penny. See if you can find the answers to the puzzle questions below on the penny. Watch out. Some of the questions are pretty tricky!

Can you find . . .
1. the name of a country?
2. a fruit?
3. a large body of water?
4. a messenger?
5. a beverage?
6. a rabbit?
7. flowers?
8. part of a river?
9. a statement of faith?
10. a part of corn?
11. a layer of paint?
12. a sacred place?

Answers:
1. America
2. date
3. C (sea)
4. one cent (one sent)
5. T (tea)
6. hair (hare)
7. two lips (tulips)
8. mouth
9. In God We Trust
10. ear
11. coat
12. temple

Try this puzzle on a friend.

22
Sand Pictures

Sand pictures are fun because you can enjoy touching them as well as seeing them.

You can get the sand you need from a backyard sandbox or a visit to the beach.

Materials:
    sand
    glue in a squeeze bottle
    drawing paper
    colored paper
    lightweight cardboard

Use the squeeze bottle of glue to carefully sketch your design on a piece of drawing paper.

Gently sprinkle sand onto the drawing paper. Then shake off the extra sand into a container. Save the extra sand for other pictures.

Let your sand picture dry before mounting it on the lightweight cardboard.

Instead of drawing paper, you can use colored paper to make a sand picture. Again, just squeeze on the glue where you want the sand to stick. Sprinkle sand on the colored paper and shake off the extra.

23
Count in Spanish

Did any of your ancestors come from Spain or Latin America?

Do you have any Spanish-speaking friends?

Learning a foreign language can be fun. Try counting to ten in Spanish. The middle column shows the Spanish words for the numbers from 1 to 10. The right-hand column will help you pronounce the Spanish words.

1	uno	oo-noh	6	seis	sayees
2	dos	dohs	7	siete	syay-tay
3	tres	trays	8	ocho	oh-choh
4	cuatro	kwah-tro	9	nueve	nway-vay
5	cinco	seen-ko	10	diez	dyays

JULY

24
Journal Writing

Journals are written records that people keep. In their journals, people write about what they do and how they feel. A journal is a private, personal record of a person's life and thoughts.

Writing something in a journal can be just like talking to someone. Haven't you ever wanted to tell someone something but the person either wasn't around or was too busy to talk? Your journal can be your best friend at such times.

To begin your journal, all you need is a notebook and a pencil or a pen. Write down the date before you begin each journal entry. By writing down the date, you create a record that you can look back at later. The date and the description will help you remember something you did or a feeling you experienced on a particular day.

25
Knox Blocks Zoo

Even if you seldom eat meat, you'll love eating these animals!

Materials:
    3-ounce package of gelatin dessert—any flavor
    1 envelope Knox gelatin
    water
    2 bowls
    9×2-inch cake pan
    cookie cutters in zoo animal shapes

Soften the Knox gelatin by mixing it with two tablespoons of water in one bowl. In the other bowl, mix the flavored gelatin dessert according to package directions and then add three tablespoons of water.

Add the Knox mixture to the flavored gelatin mixture. Pour the combined mixture into the cake pan and refrigerate until set. That usually takes about two hours.

When the mixture is set, use the cookie cutters to cut it into zoo animal shapes. Eat and enjoy!

26
Sponge Painting

Have you ever used a sponge instead of a brush to paint a picture? You can get effects with a sponge that are not possible with a brush.

Materials:
- newspapers
- smock (an old adult-size shirt works fine)
- paint (poster paints work best)
- paper
- container of water
- sponges

Start by covering a large flat work area with newspaper. Put on a smock to keep your clothes clean.

You can use sponges of different sizes, or you can cut or tear sponges into different shapes.

Wet each sponge as you plan to use it, and squeeze out the extra water. Then dip the sponge gently in the paint. Pat it on a piece of scrap paper to get rid of the extra paint.

Pat the sponge on your painting paper wherever you want that color to appear. To make a colorful design, you can use many pieces of sponge to apply several different colors.

Keep in mind that colors will lighten as you keep patting the sponge onto your paper.

When you finish your sponge painting, let the paper dry. Then frame your painting and hang it for display.

You can make your own decorated note paper by folding sheets of paper in half and sponge painting the front side. To make matching envelopes, paint the back flap of envelopes with the same design you use on your note paper.

JULY

27
Creepy Critters

Can you find the creepy critters listed below in the puzzle grid? The names are spelled forward, backward, up, down, and diagonally.

ALIENS	GIANTS	SHARKS
BATS	GOBLINS	SNAKES
BEES	GREMLINS	SPIDERS
BUGS	JAWS	TARANTULAS
CLONES	KING KONG	TROLLS
DRACULA	MARTIANS	VAMPIRES
DRAGONS	MICE	WEREWOLVES
FRANKENSTEIN	MONSTERS	WITCHES
FROGS	MUMMIES	WORMS
GHOSTS	RATS	ZOMBIES

JULY

```
S E E B R N P E L M C D X D W S A E T V L B
A B S T A R B M A I A C B N O A C P B A X C
T S L R S E N O L C Y T O S E I M M U M V Y
O R A S R W D M U E N N Q N S M R O W P M S
D E L E A S Z L C W C F P L A P J S K I D E
M T U G R F S T A B R G B V X N O G A R D I
I S H T A P C E R M B W N L O E P O P E Z B
S N I L M E R G D Q L I Y S L K X R N S T M
U O G F W I C D Y X C T S O P L U F B A N O
J M B V J K E K D A D C B V S I L Y O X V Z
N E F J H A M W S X E H N D K Y D C H C L A
S I X M A L I E N S P E M S O X S E Y E O S
Q S E A F G L W A E B S C X S M G L R Y N S
L N I T A L U H K V L A E K T H P M L S F A
S I S W S I T M E G U S R V D E A M V O D L
R L T X B N L J S P E A F G L L G R O G R U
S B S P U P E D Y H H O W O U O N U K C A T
T O O Z G C L K C S Y A J X H O W F N S G N
N G H W S I M T N X P I B J T O R E L W O A
A N G S N A I T R A M W N T C A L G R V N R
I S W A J W A P L E R C D D V M D L H E S A
G W H S O T H G S S O F G N O K G N I K W T
```

Can you think of other creepy critters or creatures?

28
It Really Bugs Me!

Are there some things that people do that really bother you?

Have you ever told anyone about these things?

Here's a chance to make a list of everything that bugs you.

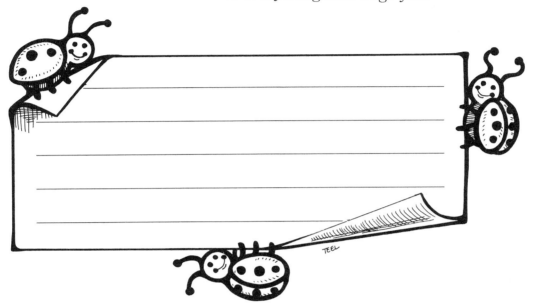

Ask a friend to make a list of the things that bug him or her. Then compare lists. Do some of the same things appear on both lists?

Choose the one thing from your list that bothers you the most. Draw a small bug next to it.

29
Collecting Coins

See if you can find the following coins with the year of your birth on each one:

penny   nickel   dime   quarter   half dollar   silver dollar

Try finding a penny, nickel, dime, quarter, and half dollar with *this year's* date on each one.

30 Gramblers

A grambler is a sentence that makes a funny connection between a quote and the person speaking.

You can use adverbs to form gramblers. An adverb is a word that tells how, when, or where. Most adverbs end with the letters "ly."

Here are some examples of gramblers with adverbs:

"There goes the steam roller," said Tom flatly.

"I'll see what I can dig up for you," said Jim gravely.

Here are some other gramblers. These make a funny connection between the quote and a person's occupation.

"That was a close shave," said Mr. Warner, the barber.

"I'm stuffed," said Mr. Smith, the taxidermist.

"That joke is so funny, I'm in stitches," said Mr. Jones, the tailor.

Now try writing some gramblers of your own.

---

31 Balloon Volleyball

Are you a great volleyball player? With this game, you can play volleyball even when the weather keeps you inside.

Use a large inflated balloon for the volleyball.

Line up several chairs to serve as the net.

Follow regular volleyball rules with one exception: Players must remain on their knees at all times!

1
Jigsaw Puzzle

Putting a jigsaw puzzle together can be fun and challenging. For even more challenging fun, try making your own jigsaw puzzle.

Materials:
   magazines
   lightweight cardboard
   scissors
   pencil
   glue

Look through magazines for interesting pictures or scenes. Choose one picture that you like best.

Glue the magazine picture to the cardboard. Make sure that the entire picture is glued down. Let it dry.

When the glue is completely dry, turn the picture over so that the cardboard side is facing up. Use a pencil to divide the cardboard into interesting shapes. Then cut along the lines you drew.

Scramble the pieces. Then try to put your puzzle together. When you're finished, store the puzzle pieces in an envelope.

2
Wheels

Look around your house for all of the objects that have wheels. Make a list of the objects. Your list will probably include such things as a bicycle, tricycle, car, lawnmower, doll buggy, wheelbarrow, skateboard, roller skates, wagon, and toy cars.

Now divide your list to show which objects have one wheel, two wheels, three wheels, and four wheels. You could even turn your list into a chart by drawing pictures of the objects in each group.

Go through old magazines to find pictures of objects that have wheels. Cut out the pictures and use them to make a display. Be sure to label each object in your display.

Use construction paper to make models of some of your favorite wheeled objects.

3
People Search

One way to get to know other people is to ask them questions.

You can do a people search by yourself or with a friend. Get started by making a list of questions. These questions will help you find people who are unusual in some way.

Here are some ideas for questions to ask:

> Can you ride a unicycle?
> Do you sleep in a bunk bed?
> Did you move to this neighborhood from another state?
> Do you have an unusual collection or hobby? If so, what is it?
> Are you a computer freak?
> Do you love vanilla ice cream?
> Can you name the Presidents of the United States in order?
> Have you ever eaten snails (escargot)?
> Are you over six feet tall?
> Have you taken a trip over 1,000 miles from home?
> Can you laugh for three minutes without stopping?
> Can you say the letters of the alphabet backwards?
> Do you have a pet skunk?
> Do you have six toes on one foot?

Keep searching until you get a yes answer to each of your questions. Ask each person who gives you a yes answer to sign his or her name next to the question that tells how he or she is unusual.

4
Mold Garden

You can grow your very own mold garden.

Materials:
  piece of bread
  plate
  large glass jar or bowl

Place the piece of bread on the plate. Moisten it with a few drops of water. Be sure not to soak the bread.

Let the bread stand uncovered in the air for about one hour. Then cover the bread with the glass jar. Put the covered bread in a dark place. A closed cupboard works well.

Look at the bread from day to day. You should soon see a mass of tiny white threads covering the bread. Shortly after the threads appear, they will change from white to some color. Usually the threads change to black or blue, but they may become a pale pink.

5
Count in French

Did any of your ancestors come from France?

Do you have any French-speaking friends?

Learning a foreign language can be fun. Try counting to ten in French. The middle column shows the French words for the numbers from 1 to 10. The right-hand column will help you pronounce the French words.

1	un	uhn		6	six	seess
2	duex	duh		7	sept	seht
3	trois	trwah		8	huit	ew-eet
4	quartre	KAH-truh		9	neuf	nuhf
5	cinq	senk		10	dix	deess

6
Your Perfect Bedroom

Think of your bedroom. How would you really like it to look?

What kind of furniture would you like it to have? What colors would you use?

What would be your favorite thing in your perfect bedroom?

Design the bedroom that would be just right for you.

Materials:
   drawing paper
   pencil
   ruler

7
Magazine Montage

A montage is a composite picture made by combining several different pictures. You can make your own montage.

Materials:
   magazines
   colored tissue paper
   glue (thinned with water)
   flat paint brush
   heavy cardboard
   felt-tipped marker
   shellac

Sort through the magazines for several pictures relating to the same subject. For example, look for pictures that show automobiles, animals, babies, or food.

Organize your group of related pictures into an attractive design. Fill in the empty spaces between pictures with colored tissue paper.

Now, using the flat brush to apply the thinned glue, glue your pictures and tissue paper to the heavy cardboard. Then let your montage dry completely.

When your montage is dry, outline some of the overlapping shapes with a felt-tipped marker. If you wish, you can put a thick coat of shellac over your entire design.

When your montage is dry, hang it up for others to enjoy.

8
Blueprints

You can make interesting blueprints with leaves.

Materials:
    sheets of blueprint paper
    piece of glass the size of the blueprint paper
    various leaves

Start by placing a leaf on a sheet of blueprint paper. Be sure to put it on the coated side of the paper. When you have the leaf arranged the way you want it, cover the leaf and paper with the glass to hold everything in place.

Carefully move the glass, leaf, and blueprint paper into the sun. Leave everything in the sun for one minute. If you don't have a watch, count to 60 slowly.

Now remove the glass and leaf from the paper. Then *immediately* wash the blueprint paper in cold running water. After you wash the paper, the part that the leaf covered will be white. The rest of the paper will be bright blue. With a thin leaf, you might be able to see the veins of the leaf on the paper.

Dry the blueprint paper by first placing it between paper towels and then putting the towels and paper between two books.

You can mount your leaf blueprint. You can also make blueprints of other objects and compare the results.

AUGUST

⑨ Turn Off the Lights

Talk with your family about ways to save electricity. Set up a system of rewards for family members who remember to turn off lights when they leave a room. Get a large jar of candy or peanuts or some other treat that everyone enjoys to use as a reward.

Keep a record (for at least one week) of the number of times lights are left on in a room when no one is there. Give the family member a treat each time he or she remembers to turn off the lights. Don't forget to reward yourself!

⑩ Toothpick Design

You can use toothpicks to create a realistic picture or an abstract design.

Materials:
> toothpicks (flat, round, or colored)
> dark-colored construction paper
> white glue

Arrange toothpicks on the construction paper in different patterns until you find the one you like best. When you have your favorite picture or design, glue the toothpicks to the paper one at a time.

Place a drop of glue on one side of the toothpick, smooth the glue over the length of the toothpick, and place the toothpick on the paper. Continue until all of the toothpicks are glued in place.

To use your toothpick design for a greeting card, start by folding the construction paper in half. Glue your design to the front side of the folded paper.

11
Nature Art

Nature is full of beautiful and interesting things that you can recycle into art objects.

Materials:
- pop-top ring (for picture hanger)
- glue
- nature materials (These are just suggestions; you can think of many more.)

driftwood	dried corn	seeds
wood	pods	shells
twigs	pine cones	dried flowers
tree bark	acorns	sand
rocks		

It would be a good idea to work on this project outdoors or in a garage. Be sure to cover your work area with newspaper.

Use a piece of tree bark or rough wood as a base. You can leave it as it is or stain it. Food coloring mixed with water will give you a light stain. If you want the base to be shiny, give it a coating of shellac.

Arrange seeds, beans, acorns, pine cones, parts of twigs, or other small items on the base until you have a design that you like. Plan your design carefully. Don't glue anything until you are entirely pleased with the arrangement.

When you have the design you like best, glue each item in place. Allow everything to dry completely. You can then place your nature art on a table or glue a hanger to the back of the base and hang it on a wall.

You can use this same method to make interesting animals or imaginary creatures on your tree bark or rough wood base. Glue rocks and pebbles of different sizes and shapes to create the animals.

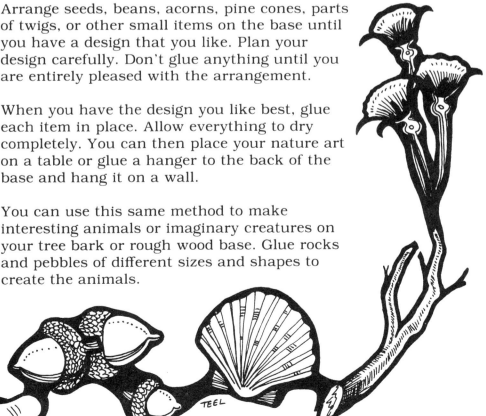

AUGUST

12
Riddles

A riddle is a question that poses a problem for someone to solve. You can find plenty of riddle books at your public library.

Do you know the answers to these riddles? If not, you'll find the answers at the bottom of the page. Try the riddles on your friends.

1. What is the most useless when it is full?
2. What has 88 keys but cannot open a door?
3. What starts with "e" and ends with "e" and has one letter in it?
4. What has a cap but never takes it off?
5. What belongs to you but others use it more than you do?
6. What room can you never go into?
7. What animal never plays fair?
8. What Roman numeral can climb a wall?
9. What bird can lift the heaviest weights?
10. What two letters mean "not difficult"?

Answers:
1. a wastebasket
2. a piano
3. an envelope
4. a knee
5. your name
6. a mushroom
7. a cheetah
8. IV
9. the crane
10. E Z

Straw Painting

Here's a fun way to make an art project.

Materials:
- plastic straws
- paper
- poster paint
- newspaper
- old spoon

Start by covering your work area with newspaper.

Use an old spoon to place a blob of paint anywhere on a piece of paper.

Place one end of a straw near the blob of paint. *Gently* blow into the other end of the straw. The paint will spread into different designs. Let the paint dry completely. Then hang your painting for others to enjoy.

You can make straw paintings with two or three colors of paint. You can also use a paper plate instead of paper for your straw painting.

Flour Clay

You can make your own clay. Here's the recipe.

Ingredients:
- 1 cup flour
- 1 cup salt
- 1 rounded teaspoon powdered alum (available at drugstores)

Mix the flour, salt, and alum together in a bowl. Knead until the mixture reaches a clay-like consistency.

You can use this homemade clay exactly like real clay. Be creative. Use the flour clay to make animals, bowls, miniature toys, and other things you like.

If you wrap the flour clay in a wet cloth, it will keep for a few days.

AUGUST

15
Clouds

There are four main types of clouds. Their names come from ancient Latin words.

Cumulus—means heap or pile.
  These clouds are closest to Earth. Thick cumulus clouds are flat on the bottom and appear to be piled high on top like a fluffy dome.

Stratus—means spread out.
  These are thin flat clouds. They are always flat on both the bottom and the top. Stratus clouds can cover hundreds of miles on hazy, drizzly days when there is little sunlight.

Cirrus—means curl.
  These feathery clouds are like wispy curls of white hair. They are the highest clouds, reaching up to 10 miles above the Earth. Although they appear to travel slowly, cirrus clouds can move at speeds of 100 to 200 miles per hour.

Nimbus—means rainstorm.
  These are the clouds that make thunderstorms and hail. Thunderheads develop from cumulo-nimbus clouds.

Go outside and look at the sky. What kind of clouds do you see?

You might want to keep a record of the different types of clouds you see for a week or a month.

16
Poetry—Cinquain

A cinquain is a French poem. Cinq is the French word for five, and a cinquain always has five lines. In addition, each line of the poem must have a certain number of words.

Line 1 has one word that gives the title.
Line 2 has two words.   [Lines 2–4
Line 3 has three words.   tell about
Line 4 has four words.   the title.]
Line 5 has one word that summarizes the idea.

Here's a cinquain that I wrote:

Girls
Playing games,
Making up stories,
Laughing and singing,
Happy.

Nancy E. Velon

Try writing some cinquains on your own. You can use a variety of titles. Here are some ideas: animals, colors, toys, people, feelings, places.

17
Orange Freeze

Here's the recipe for a great summertime refresher.

Ingredients:
1 6-ounce can frozen orange juice concentrate
1 cup skim milk
½ teaspoon vanilla
½ cup sugar
10 to 12 ice cubes

Put all of the ingredients into a blender. Blend for 30 to 40 seconds.

Pour the orange freeze into glasses. This recipe serves four to six people.

Reproduced with permission.
©*Children's Help Your Heart Cookbook*, 1980.
Copyright American Heart Association.

Word Pictures

Words help us tell our ideas to other people. The way a word is written can help you understand its meaning. The words below are written as word pictures to show the meanings of the words.

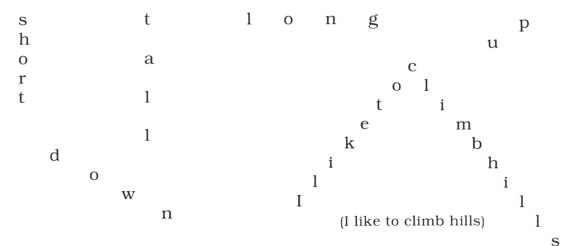

(I like to climb hills)

Try making some word pictures on your own.

Recycled Greeting Cards

Do you have an old box of Christmas or greeting cards around the house? You can turn the cards into new and interesting things.

You can cut out the pictures to decorate gift boxes. Or you can use them to make name tags for your next party.

Here are some other ideas:

> Make place cards for a Sunday dinner. Put a card next to the place where each person will sit.
>
> Find a Christmas or greeting card with a pretty scene. Cut out the scene, and cut out a paper frame for the scene. Hang the framed scene on the wall.
>
> Find a pretty picture, cut it out from the card, and glue it on a paper plate. Punch a hole in the top of the plate. Tie a loop of yarn through the hole, and hang the decorated paper plate in the kitchen or a window.

Think of some other ways to make interesting items out of old cards.

20
Magnet Magic

A magnet is a piece of metal that attracts things made of iron.

The first magnets were discovered over 2,000 years ago. Shepherds in an ancient country called Magnesia discovered that certain rocks stuck to the iron ends of their staffs. These hard, black lodestones had a pulling power that attracted metal. Some people in Magnesia thought the stones were magical.

Today's magnets are much like lodestone. Our magnets have two opposite poles: the north pole and the south pole. The poles of a magnet are of equal strength.

The largest magnet is the Earth. No one knows exactly what causes magnetism.

If an item is heavy and contains iron, a magnet will stick to it. A magnet will pick up lightweight metal items like paper clips, nails, and tacks.

How many other things can you find that a magnet will pick up?

AUGUST

21 Seed Pictures

You can create an interesting picture using different seeds and dried beans. Seeds and beans come in a variety of sizes, shapes, and colors.

Materials:
    heavy drawing paper or cardboard
    glue
    a variety of seeds and beans—lima, pinto, and navy beans,
        dried corn and peas, popcorn, and rice

Use a pencil to outline your scene or design on the drawing paper or cardboard.

Fill in your outline with a variety of seeds and beans. Glue the seeds and beans to the paper or cardboard. Use enough glue so that the seeds and beans stick securely. The glue will turn clear when it dries.

If you like, you can cover your picture with a thin coat of shellac or spray it with clear plastic.

22 Musical Glasses

Have you always wanted to play a musical instrument? Here's your chance to play a melody with drinking glasses and water!

Gather several glasses of equal size. Instead of drinking glasses, you can use jelly or canning jars or other glass containers.

Place the various glasses or jars on the table. Then fill them with different amounts of water. The less water in the glass, the higher the note. The more water you add, the lower the note will be.

Gently tap each glass or jar with a spoon and listen to the sound.

Arrange the glasses or jars from lowest to highest sound.

Now see if you can tap out a simple song such as "Twinkle, Twinkle, Little Star." Then try your hand at playing more difficult tunes.

23
Scavenger Hunt

Have a scavenger hunt in your house, garage, or yard. Try to find the items listed below. If you have the hunt with a friend, you may also search his or her house, garage, and yard for the items.

- ☆ peanut with its shell on
- ☆ buffalo-head nickel
- ☆ four-leaf clover
- ☆ striped shoelaces
- ☆ leaf from an ivy plant
- ☆ wooden spoon
- ☆ penny with the year you were born on it
- ☆ bird's feather
- ☆ seashell
- ☆ the spice called rosemary (look in the kitchen)
- ☆ 20 raisins (to eat later)
- ☆ silver dollar
- ☆ wooden spool (thread comes on spools)
- ☆ the nine of clubs (a playing card)
- ☆ a baby tooth (not in someone's mouth!)
- ☆ your favorite toy as a baby
- ☆ a postage stamp from another country
- ☆ a chicken bone

HAVE FUN!

24
Baker's Clay

You cannot eat baker's clay, but you can use it to make many interesting shapes. It's a handy dough to use for making Christmas ornaments.

Here's the recipe for baker's clay.

Ingredients:
- 4 cups unsifted all-purpose flour
- 1 cup salt
- 1½ cups water

Use a spoon to mix all the ingredients together in a bowl. Then mix them thoroughly with your hands. If the mixture is too stiff, add just a bit more water.

Remove the dough from the bowl, and place it on a clean surface.

Knead the dough for at least five minutes (ten minutes is better).

Shape the dough into the forms you want.

Bake the dough forms on a cookie sheet in a preheated oven set to 350°. Remove the cookie sheet when the forms are golden brown. Baking usually takes from 15 to 45 minutes, depending on the thickness of the shapes. Check your shapes from time to time while they're baking to know when to remove them from the oven.

After you take the cookie sheet out of the oven, remove the shapes and allow them to cool.

When the shapes are completely cooled, you can decorate them with acrylic paints.

25
Hot-Dish Trivet

A trivet is placed under a hot dish to protect the table from being damaged by the heat. A trivet may be made of metal, wood, or ceramic.

You can make your own hot-dish trivet by following these instructions.

Materials:
- 15 ice cream bar sticks
- heavy cardboard
- glue
- poster paints
- shellac or clear plastic spray

Gather eight of the ice cream sticks, and paint one side of them with poster paint. Leave the other seven sticks plain. Allow the painted sticks to dry.

When the painted sticks are dry, lay all the sticks on the heavy cardboard so that the painted ones and plain ones alternate—first a painted, then a plain, then a painted, and so on. The sticks will form a rectangle.

Make an outline of the sticks on the cardboard. Cut the cardboard to the size of this rectangle.

Glue the sticks in place on the cardboard. Place a heavy object on the sticks until they have completely dried in place.

When the glue is dry, the hot-dish trivet is ready for use. If you like, you can brush on a thin coat of shellac or spray on a coat of clear plastic. If you use one of these finishes, allow time for it to dry before using the trivet.

As a variation, you can paint all the sticks. Then alternate colors to create a pleasing pattern.

26
Tangrams

A tangram is a Chinese puzzle made up of seven pieces.

You can make your own tangram by tracing the seven pieces below onto a piece of paper. Carefully cut out each piece. Arrange the pieces of your tangram to make different shapes and designs.

27
Make an Organic Garden

Plants need soil in order to grow. Soil supports the plant, stores moisture for it, and provides the chemicals that the plant needs to make food.

You can make your own mini-garden that uses only natural (organic) items.

Materials:
    large empty jar or coffee can
    coffee grounds (from the morning's breakfast)
    newspaper
    orange peels, apple peels, or dried leaves
    dry cereal, crushed
    plant seeds or beans

Put the coffee grounds in the bottom of the empty jar or coffee can. Shred a large sheet of newspaper into tiny pieces and place them on top of the coffee grounds.

Break the orange peels (or apple peels or dried leaves) into small pieces and add them to the jar or can. Then add a handful of the crushed cereal.

Stir up the mixture and moisten it with water.

Cover the jar or can. Punch several small holes in the top.

Let the jar or can sit in a warm place for several days. Examine the contents daily. Note how the mixture looks and smells. At the end of one week, stir up the soil until it is well mixed.

Plant some seeds or beans in the soil. Place the jar or can—with the cover off—in a window. Keep the soil moist, but do not add too much water.

Watch your plant grow. Water it (just a little) every few days.

28
Board Games

Invite some friends over to play board games. Ask each friend to bring a game.

Here are some favorite board games:

<pre>
          Checkers   Clue
                    Monopoly
                                                        Yahtzee
          Chinese Checkers
                              Risk
  Chess
                         Bargain Hunter
             Sorry   Easy Money
                         Life
          Scrabble   Payday
</pre>

Serve lemonade or some other refreshment.

If you want to give out prizes to the winners, gather some comic books, baseball cards, marbles, or snack treats.

29
Good Luck Box

Many people believe that certain objects will bring them success or good luck. You can make a collection of objects that bring you good luck.

Materials:
    container—shoe box, coffee can, metal tin, or small wooden box
    lucky charms—rabbit's foot, penny, shell, something red, silver spoon, something with the number 7 on it, something in the shape of a triangle

Find as many good luck charms as you can. You can use the list above, but be sure to add your own lucky charms to your collection.

Ask friends what objects bring them good luck. Add these items to your collection, too. You might even help your friends start their own good luck boxes.

AUGUST

30
Back to School

Summer vacation will soon be over.

Did you make some new friends?

Did you have fun trying some new ideas?

Did you find out something interesting about yourself?

Have you done your "back to school" shopping?

Have you given some thought to what your new year in school will be like?

If you could create your own perfect school, what would it be?

    What type of building would you choose?

    What kind of furniture and desks would you want?

    Would any of the teachers be the real teachers at your actual school?

    How would you get from room to room?

    What would come out of the drinking fountains?

    What special things would be on the playground?

    How would you arrive at school each day?

    What new things would you learn?

Write a description of your new school and a story about your first day there.

Make a large drawing of your perfect school.

AUGUST

31
Hang Loose

AUGUST

RELAX—in your favorite chair.

RELAX—in a swing.

RELAX—under your favorite tree.

RELAX—in bed.

RELAX—in the pool.

RELAX—hanging out with your favorite friend.

RELAX—and think about all your summer fun! Share your thoughts with someone in your family.